LIFE LESSONS FROM THE
OCEAN

With thanks to Alex,
Alasdair, Ivor and Travis.

First published in Great Britain in 2020 by LOM ART, an imprint of
Michael O'Mara Books Limited
9 Lion Yard
Tremadoc Road
London SW4 7NQ

A CIP catalogue record for this book is available from the British Library.

Papers used by Michael O'Mara Books Limited are natural, recyclable
products made from wood grown in sustainable forests. The manufacturing
processes conform to the environmental regulations of the country of origin.

ISBN: 978-1-910552-99-5 in hardback print format
ISBN: 978-1-912785-26-1 in ebook format

1 2 3 4 5 6 7 8 9 10

Designed by Ana Bjezancevic and Barbara Ward
Printed and bound in China

www.mombooks.com

MIX
Paper from
responsible sources
FSC® C016973
FSC
www.fsc.org

LIFE LESSONS FROM THE
OCEAN

Soothing Wisdom
from the Sea

Written by Richard Harrington
Illustrated by Annie Davidson

Introduction

GET YOUR FEET WET IN THE OCEAN

Life began in the sea, just a few billion years ago. Now the ocean shapes our lives without us realizing it, stabilizing our climate and providing oxygen to breathe. But it gives us so much more: food, travel, fun. Just being by it influences our mood and state of mind. It has powers to refresh, give perspective and take away the pressures of life. Its untiring motion is tied with our own daily rhythms, influenced by the moon and sun. We've come to realize how fragile and damaged it has become, but the more we know the more we can do to repair it. And if you spend just a little time by, on or under the waves, learning more about it becomes simply addictive. The sea has so much to say; as you pick through these pages, you'll discover the secrets and gems that lie beneath.

Small is important

~

The mightiest living creature, for its importance
to the fabric of life in and around the ocean, is the
very smallest. Tiny plant plankton abound in large
numbers near the sea's surface, turning sunlight and
carbon dioxide into energy, and releasing oxygen. They
provide over half of the oxygen we breathe. Unlike
plants with roots, phytoplankton move freely around,
and many have the most stunning shapes and forms
to help them float and drift. In large numbers, they
colour the sea in reds or greens and some, like the sea
sparkle, give off light themselves, making a beautiful
glowing spectacle through spring and summer nights.

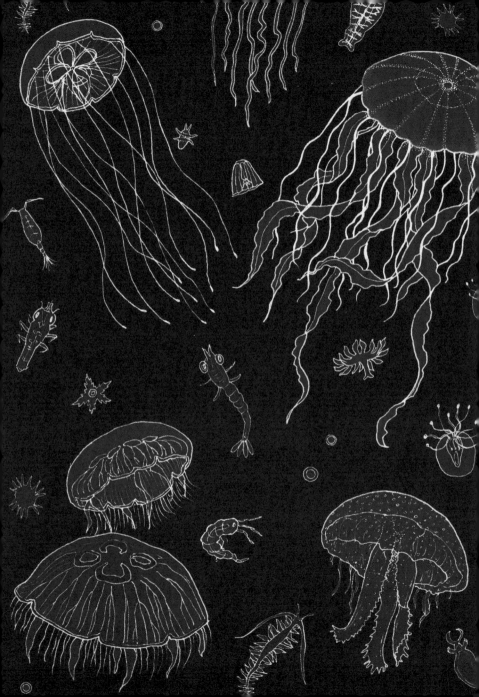

It's OK to be a drifter

∞

Among the floating plant plankton a legion of animals
dwell. A huge number of fish, crabs, lobsters and snails
start life as tiny floating creatures that barely resemble
their later, fully grown forms. Some worms, crustaceans
and molluscs stay in this floating world for their whole
lives. While most are small, giant jellyfish drift among
this zooplankton. Enormous leatherback turtles and
ocean sunfish feed on jellies, and the biggest animals on
earth – like great whales and whale sharks – swallow
up the rich soup of plankton by the giant mouthful.

Take comfort in those around you

∾

The sea is home to many kinds of animals that have no relatives out of water. Take the bryozoans, or moss animals. These are tiny creatures that live in colonies on rocks and weeds in the sea, often looking more like a mat or carpet. But many grow to look like weeds, such as the hornwrack and the sea chervil. Most are harmless, but eczema-like symptoms on the skin of sea fishermen, who handle sea chervil among fishing gear, are caused by a chemical in the bryozoan.

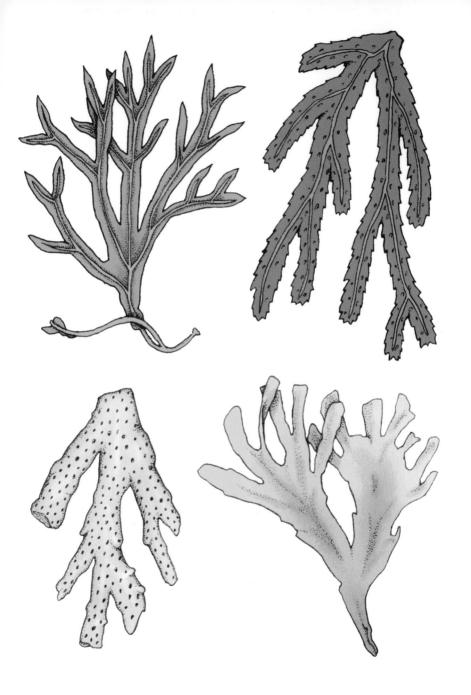

Take your role in life seriously

∞

Sponges have been harvested by people for thousands of years, until synthetic versions replaced them. There is an astounding number of different forms of sponge, all made up of the building blocks of very small, very simple animals. In many sponges the tiny animals in different parts of a colony perform specific tasks, some bringing in food-containing water, others filtering it, and still more passing waste products out again – each individual animal will do no other role for the colony, yet will work harmoniously with others.

Take time to breathe

~

Imagine being a sea fish, left high and dry by the tide.
This can happen twice every day, with wind, freshwater
rain, and hot sunshine added. It sounds terrible, but
this is what the common blenny, or shanny, thrives on.
The fish can be encountered tens of feet above the
low tideline, and if you peer into holes and crevices in
rocks you're sure to find one within a short time. While
the fish must keep moist, it can take in air through
its skin, and gulps air through its mouth too. It can
stay alive for several days out of water. As soon as the
tide returns, it can get back to swimming, feeding and
taking its oxygen from the water like any other fish.

See the wonder in the world around you

The Arctic is a wonderland of ice and snow, sitting on an ocean of amazing life. Fantastic creatures that seem mythical thrive here. An overgrown tooth on the front of a narwhal makes a single horn or tusk that can be two thirds as long as the animal itself. Most males grow one and some females develop one too. The tusk has many uses, helping to catch prey on deep-diving search parties for large fish near the seabed, and narwhals rub tusks on greeting each other. Being a tooth, the tusk is very sensitive, and may help the narwhal detect changes in the water and air around it.

It pays to be patient

⁓

Anglerfish are bizarre and monstrous-looking creatures but they are fascinating. Most lie still on the seabed, dangling a pointy appendage on the top of the head to entice prey. Anglers in the deep ocean, known as ceratoid anglers, attract prey with a luminescent lure. Small fish find the bright light irresistible, swim closer to investigate and – with one gulp – the angler has its meal. Finding a mate can take a long time too, and when it happens, a male angler might stay with the much larger female for the remainder of his life.

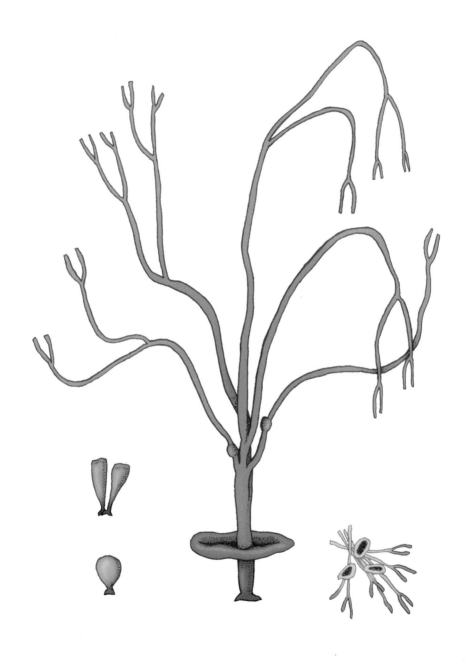

Prepare for times of turbulence

Seaweeds cannot grow roots on rocks like plants do
in soil, and instead each weed anchors itself to the
sea floor with a strong sticky pad, called a holdfast.
A seaweed can grow tall from this base and withstand
most sea conditions in summer. But the bigger it
grows, the greater the danger that storms and currents
will dislodge it. Seaweeds are often home to grazing
animals like limpets and urchins, making them heavier
and even more likely to be ripped away by currents.
Bigger seaweeds tend to grow and then die back each
year before winter, so miss damaging seasonal storms.

Put your roots down in calm waters

～

Some plants can grow in seawater. Seagrasses live among sand and mud where they can put down roots. They need lots of sunlight to grow and so are only found in shallow, clear water that tends to stay undisturbed by storms. Vast underwater meadows of seagrasses called *posidonia* grow around the Mediterranean, making a habitat for seahorses, flatfish such as stingray, and anemones. When their leaves do break off, the rolling motion of the sea turns them into soft balls that wash up on beaches, often forming piles of material that provide nutrients for plants to grow on land.

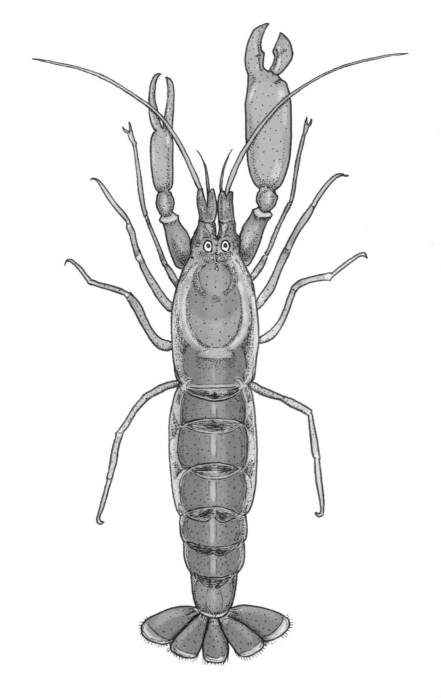

Love your noisy neighbours

Snapping shrimps have an ingenious mechanism in one
of their two claws. The giant claw, which can be half
of the body length of the shrimp, makes an explosive
bang, intense enough to stun their prey if it is close by.
Together, the shrimps make a raucous symphony that
can be heard for tens of metres around. Where these
noisy shrimps are present, the reef is usually healthy,
and it has been discovered that young fish choose to
move into reefs that have lots of shrimp sounds going
on. It just shows that a healthy home is a noisy one.

Find your niche in life

❧

Competition for space on a coral reef is fierce. Each species of coral is in a struggle for prime real estate with its neighbours. They need a constant supply of food – tiny plankton – and they also need clear water and sunlight. This is because the corals that build reefs get extra food by hosting special algae among their tissues; these provide nutrients, so the corals can grow and thrive. Corals take on different forms to outgrow their neighbours – some look like antlers, others are distinctly brain-shaped, while many more have fingers and branches.

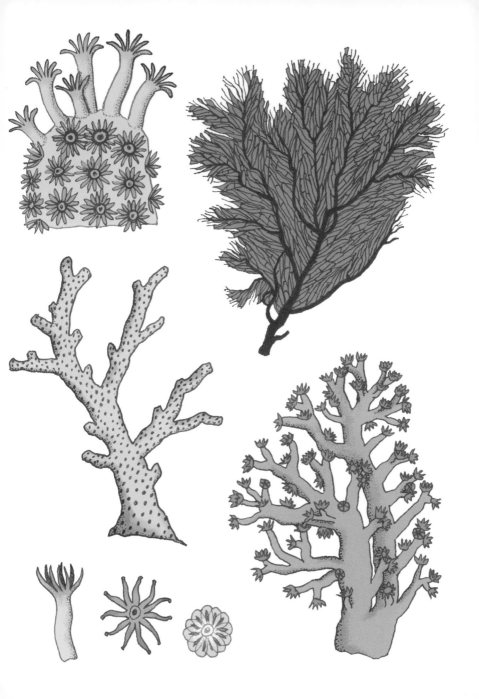

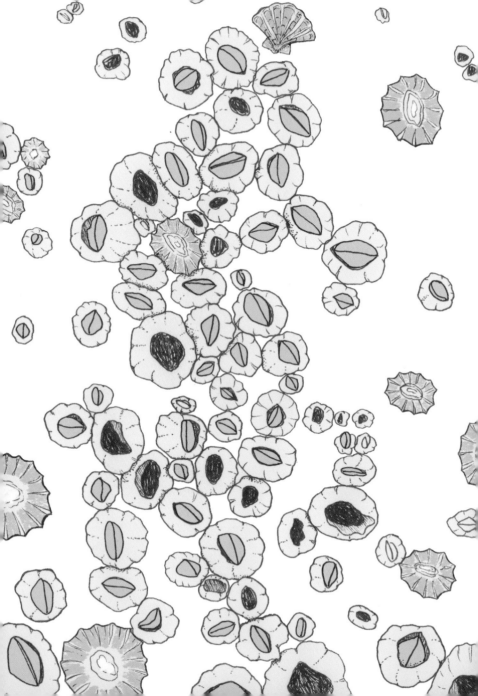

Be choosy about where you live

∞

Barnacles start life floating helplessly among plankton, changing their body shape as they grow. They are very choosy about where they settle, as an adult barnacle cannot move from its final home. The larva will drop from the water and walk around a prospective new home rock for some time until, when happy, it then cements itself, upside down, on the floor. With its legs raised above its body, all enclosed in a case of armour that includes a trapdoor, it spends the rest of its life using its fine legs to catch plankton food floating by.

Go with the ebb and the flow

࿐

Tides are caused by the pull of gravity from the moon and the sun, and the sea laps up and down the shore roughly twice daily in most places. The rhythm of the tide is set and can be predicted accurately for many years ahead. At the time of the full and new moon, when the sun and moon align, especially high and low tides, called spring tides, occur. These make the best conditions if you want to explore the shore, or just sit on a wide expanse of beach at low tide.

Don't underestimate the power of self-healing

Underneath its bumpy exterior, the common starfish hides
its strength as a real survivor. It must face the harshest of
storms and fearsome predators; even its favourite foods,
like mussels and small crabs, can inflict injury. But a
starfish doesn't let this hold it back. It can lose an entire
arm, escape quickly, and grow back a completely new
limb. In fact, it can survive losing two, three or even four
arms in one go, and be largely back to normal within
a year. Life throws occasional mishaps and accidents at
all of us, and the human body's power to recover from
a setback is amazing, too. We shouldn't let a wound
or trauma stop us doing the things we love to do.

The ocean is a healer

The sea provides us with natural therapy for mind, body and soul. While the ocean is in constant motion, this powerful, dependable force is both relaxing and thrilling in equal measure. And it is being recognized more and more that our mental health and well-being is improved by time spent in and near water. This is true whether just sitting by the sea or surfing in wild waves. Of course, it can be dangerous too, so don't get perilously close to a cliff edge, or swim beyond your capabilities. But a break spent by the sea makes you feel better – fact!

Be prepared to be surprised

∞

You may have seen flying fish, but have you ever heard
of a flying squid? As a mollusc, it is related to slugs and
snails, but the Japanese flying squid (*Todorodes pacificus*) is
anything but slow. It is jet-propelled, squirting water at
high speed through its siphon, a funnel-like tube, to push
it along. It migrates each year, travelling over 1,200 miles
at an average of three feet per second. When it puts on
a burst, it moves at ten feet per second through water
(about seven miles per hour), enough to lift it from the
sea's surface and, with less resistance from the air compared
to water, can reach up to twenty-five miles per hour and
escape any predator. You'll believe it when you see it.

Looks can be deceiving

The banded sea krait is a sea snake, with one of
the most potent venoms of all snakes. It rarely bites
humans, as its usual diet is fish and it has a very small
mouth, unsuited to biting large prey. It is certainly
best avoided; something the harmless harlequin snake
eel has evolved to take advantage of. Living in the
same places as the krait, it can swim largely without
fear of attack by predators that would probably find
it rather tasty. Mimicry is common in the underwater
world – sometimes it is hard to tell who is who.

Beauty is more than skin-deep

∞

With a face that only its mother could love, a lumpfish,
or lumpsucker, is an unlikely beast. The male is blue and
the female is brown, and both are covered in lumpy warts.
Males can be seen in sheltered pools low on the shore,
guarding eggs until they hatch. Bigger than most fish
you'll encounter in tidal pools, the male won't move, and
in fact is stuck to the seabed by a circular suction disc,
adapted from the fins on its belly. It won't move until its
eggs have hatched. It is actually a very endearing fish.

Never judge by appearances

⁓

Mud makes hippos happy, according to the song, but it makes worms, clams and fish even happier. The surface of mud can look lifeless and still, but a closer examination reveals life teeming on and beneath the surface. This mud is a food store for fish. Flatfish, like stingray, can sense the unfortunate worms just below the surface and hoover them up. Bass, grey mullet and herring will use sheltered muddy shallows as nursery grounds and may rarely leave a good location as the juveniles grow fast on nutritious worms.

Worms can be beautiful

Worms are vital in the ecology of the undersea world,
but here there are many exquisite and intriguing forms.
Take the Christmas tree worm. Its body lies hidden
in holes in coral reefs, but when it feeds, it sends out
feathery tentacles that look fir-tree shaped, with added
glistening decorations, too. The football jersey worm
sports attractive stripes – its longer cousin, the bootlace
worm, has been reported as reaching 180 feet long.

Slugs can be even prettier

An amazing range of sea slugs take on the most
delightful and varied forms of almost any group of
animal. Names like the Spanish dancer, Spanish shawl,
and blue glaucus are grand, and in real life the slugs are
even grander. They live colourful lives, too – almost all
have male and female organs, maximizing the chances
of reproducing in a world of change and uncertainty.
Some feed on venomous animals and use the stinging
cells of their prey for their own self-defence.

Never grow old

∞

It sounds impossible, but a modest-looking clam seems to have found the formula to defeat ageing. Called an ocean quahog, this two-shelled mollusc has been shown to live healthily to at least 500 years old. Even more amazingly, the tissues of the animal show little sign of ageing compared to those of younger specimens. The secret? It seems that a life spent in a bed of soft mud, with a plentiful supply of food to filter from the seawater, does wonders. Individuals alive today may have seen Christopher Columbus sail above them!

Care for others

Humpbacks are magnificent whales, growing to over fifty feet long. Adults are too big for most predators to take on, but it takes over a decade for a whale's calf to grow to adult size. Orca, and large sharks such as tiger sharks, could kill or injure a calf, and a whale mother will care consistently for its youngster for several years, doing her utmost to ward off all predators. Humpbacks will even help others – chasing predators away from hunted seals and, on occasion, have helpfully intervened where humans have been in danger in the sea.

Find joy in language and keep in touch

∞

The sperm whale's brain is the largest and heaviest-known of any animal, inside a huge head with a toothed mouth with which it grabs its favourite food – squid. It does this at great depth, and a group of whales will keep in constant contact through loud clicks and whistles as they hunt. At the surface of the sea, they keep in touch with each other with another set of sounds, and it seems that groups in separate parts of the world's oceans use alternative dialects, almost like a different language, to communicate.

Form a strong partnership

∽

Clownfish and anemones are both very colourful,
with no way to hide from hungry predators even
among bright corals. The anemone is well armed
with stinging tentacles, and so most animals stay clear
of it. Also called anemonefish, clownfish can tolerate
anemone stings and live among the tentacles. This helps
both of them, making a safe home for the clownfish,
which chases away unwelcome anemone predators
and pests. Both are quite messy eaters, so share scraps
of food. Together, the two grow healthy and strong.

Sometimes you have to fend for yourself

∞

A grey seal pup is born in late autumn or winter in wild, cold seas. The pup is entirely dependent on its mother to stay alive and needs her rich milk to help it grow quickly. But even she must feed and will leave her pup alone on the shore for many hours at a time. Usually, the pup is left in a sheltered cove, where predators are unlikely to find it. While it may look forlorn to human eyes, the pup is a born survivor. Its thick coat is ample for any wintry weather, and soon it will shed its fluffy white fur and be ready to swim in the sea on its own.

Think differently

∽

The octopus is a surprising creature in many ways. It has three hearts, pumping blue blood around its body, and eight arms. It can change the colour of its skin, as well as the texture, in a matter of milliseconds to mimic its surroundings, or show one of its complex moods. Perhaps the most striking feature of all is its high intelligence. An octopus is inquisitive, a consummate escape artist, and has been shown through tests to have amazing memory and problem-solving abilities. More incredibly, its brain system is distributed through its arms – seemingly, its arms can think for themselves!

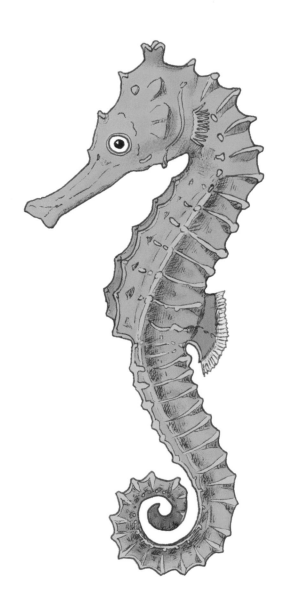

Learn to blend in

∞

There are many kinds of seahorse, from pygmy seahorses
that never grow bigger than your thumbnail, to some
species that grow over a foot long. The male broods
the eggs and hatchlings, giving birth to tiny youngsters
from a pouch on its belly. Adults and babies are always
difficult to spot, almost impossible to see among weeds,
corals and seagrass – not just for people, but also for the
tiny shrimps that seahorses eat. They can stay motionless
for long periods and move stealthily among their
surroundings before rapidly sucking up their prey.

Sometimes it pays to hide in plain sight

～

The leafy sea dragon is a seahorse-like fish that has taken
the camouflage business to an exquisite art form. With
weed-shaped appendages that make it look more like
a seaweed than an animal, it can blend invisibly among
weeds, and then can move around freely knowing it is
unlikely to be eaten when it has nothing to hide behind,
as it looks just like a piece of floating weed. A new
species of sea dragon was discovered in deeper waters
off Southern Australia in only 2015, showing just how
good a sea dragon's ability to go undetected really is!

Be ready to grasp opportunities when they come to you

The ocean floor is vast, and it can be hard to find food or meet others of your kind. At depth, it is also very, very dark. Keen senses of smell and touch, and lightning quick reactions, help creatures like the gulper eel find food. This bizarre, usually slender eel-like fish can open its jaws enormously wide to swallow prey, and its body stretches to accommodate food bigger than itself. This is helpful as it might take weeks to find another meal. The eel can also make itself bigger to frighten off predators, and some kinds give firefly-like flashes from the tail, which may attract food and mates.

Slow starters will go the distance

~

Size really matters for the leatherback turtle. All turtles
are reptiles, so are cold-blooded and need to keep
warm to be able to move. Fully grown leatherbacks
can keep their body temperature high with fatty tissues
and blood vessels close to the skin. The turtle starts
life less than ten centimetres long, and needs to keep
in warm tropical seas to start with. As it grows, it is
able to venture into cooler waters where its favourite
food, large jellyfish, can be found. They become
great ocean wanderers and roam far and wide.

Believe that you can survive anything

The marine iguana is a reptile, believed to have floated on
debris to the Galapagos Islands from its ancestral home
in central America. To survive, it learned to dive in the
sea, collecting luscious green seaweed in the shallows.
The water here is cold, and the lizards spend many
hours warming in the sun just to stay alive. Sun and salt
make for cracked skin – they also have to sneeze a lot
to get rid of saltwater from their nostrils after a dive!

Be a gentle giant

The basking shark, reaching over thirty feet in length and weighing up to seven tonnes, is the largest fish in the North Atlantic – only the whale shark beats it to the title of world's biggest fish. Giant it may be, but the basking shark won't eat you – it prefers to gorge on a rich soup of plankton. Its large, round dorsal fin can often be seen together with both the tip of the tail and the nose visible on the sea's surface, making a triple-pointed form that just might have been responsible for tales of sea serpents.

Let others groom your hard-to-reach places

The undersea world has its harmful parasites, and
fish, turtles and other creatures cannot remove lice
and other skin pests easily. These animals know they
can receive a healthy clean-up if they visit a cleaner
wrasse – a helpful fish that specializes in grooming
and de-lousing others. A wrasse can have a queue of
expectant visitors to its home spot on the reef, including
predatory sharks and groupers that leave the wrasse
unharmed in return for its services. And a good wrasse
can service more than 1,000 fish in any one day, gaining
more than enough food from the lice they nibble!

Be a strategic thinker

⌒

The killer whale, or orca, is more closely related
to dolphins than other whales and is an intelligent
predator. Orcas travel in organized pods, usually led by a
dominant female matriarch. They can live many decades
together, developing ways of hunting successfully. Orca
communicate with each other frequently until they
are hunting at close quarters; then, they often go into
a silent stealth mode to surprise their quarry. They use
diverse strategies for different prey, including rocking
hapless seals off ice floes, using their tails to force fish
into tightly packed shoals and, hunting as a pack, can
even chase and drown whales bigger than themselves.

Make good while the sun shines

Some seaweeds grow as tall as trees, even though they must grow in one short season. Giant kelp on California's coast grow at a rate of one to two feet per day in spring and summer, reaching up towards the sunlit surface from a depth of as much as 100 feet. Fortunately, the cold waters here are rich in nutrients, and float-like gas bladders help the kelp stay upright and bathed in sunlight near the surface above. Once at the surface, the fronds of the kelp keep growing, and sea otters make use of them to stay anchored in one spot as they and their babies rest.

Take time to play

~~

Sea otters are coated in a very dense fur that keeps them warm and helps them float incredibly well at the sea's surface. They can lie on their backs and break open hard shells of clams by striking them against a stone placed on their chest. They live in a harsh and dangerous environment with hunting sharks, extreme weather and strong currents to contend with. But, even as adults, sea otters take time to play, tussling and playfighting together, and toying with objects they find. They are often seen holding hands with one another as they sleep so that they do not drift apart.

The best things in life are free

Many ocean dwellers are scavengers, picking up what's left behind by others. Crabs and lobsters are experts in the art of finding food for free. The common shore crab is not a fussy eater and will eat long-dead fish, snails and worms, seaweeds and even the remains of its own kind.

A crab's shell is like an external skeleton and must be shed regularly, usually once each year. You may find a very soft crab sheltering beneath a rock and an empty 'body' nearby, which this growing individual has just stepped from. If you are lucky enough to see a crab moult, you can watch the emerged soft crab grow before your very eyes.

Softness can be a strength

⌒

Some of the softest-bodied animals in the ocean can be found in the hardest places to live. Anemones thrive where crashing waves and strong currents would dislodge and destroy almost any living thing. They stay stuck to rocks, or buried in sediments, without coming to harm. When out of water or in still conditions, they appear as shapeless blobs, but anemones can look like exquisitely beautiful flowers when they stretch out their tentacles, which they do when water moves rapidly around them. Their tentacles are lined with tiny stinging cells to trap food from the seawater, including living creatures such as shrimps or floating carrion.

Swim against the tide

Salmon are different to other fish in the sea. While they live much of their lives in salty seawater, they start and end their lives in rivers of freshwater. The Atlantic salmon starts life as a small egg hidden among gravel on a riverbed, far from the sea. To lay her eggs here, the parent salmon swam heroically against the flow, leaping step-like weirs and waterfalls. After spawning, both male and female salmon become very weak, but some survive and return to the sea once more.

Beautiful can be deadly

Some beautiful shelled snails are venomous. Called cone shells, or cone snails, they look lovely and quite harmless among sand or coral. It can be tempting to pick one up, but if you do, or just get close and disturb a living cone snail, you are in danger of being speared with a barbed harpoon, armed with a venom that has been known to kill humans. The snails use their toxic weapon to catch fish, which they eat. These sea snails have evolved to produce a range of different chemicals, including, amazingly, some that act as pain relievers now used in pain-relief drugs for humans.

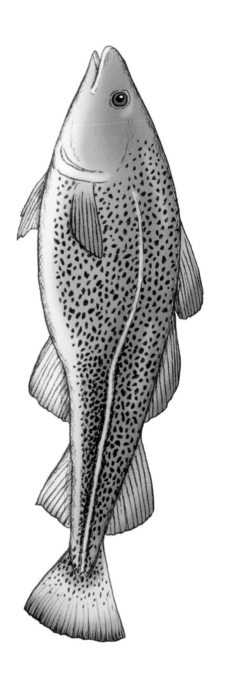

Plain can be successful

The Atlantic cod doesn't look very remarkable, but is one of the most popular fish for people to eat around the world. It is a predatory fish that lives close to the sea floor, where it feeds on smaller fish and a range of shellfish, squid and crabs. It can live to be twenty-five years or more and is a prolific breeder – a large female will produce several million tiny eggs, just over one millimetre across, at a time. Cod gather to spawn together in enormous numbers, although fishing has reduced their populations dramatically in recent decades.

Be resourceful
at mealtimes

∿

The bottlenose dolphin is a sleek, clever animal, just as comfortable in warm or cool water, and equally happy in water that is clear or murky. It can catch its food using sound waves, bouncing clicks and whistles through the water and detecting how they bounce off objects nearby. The way it makes and detects the noises isn't fully understood, but it is known that the sound comes from an organ in the head called a melon.

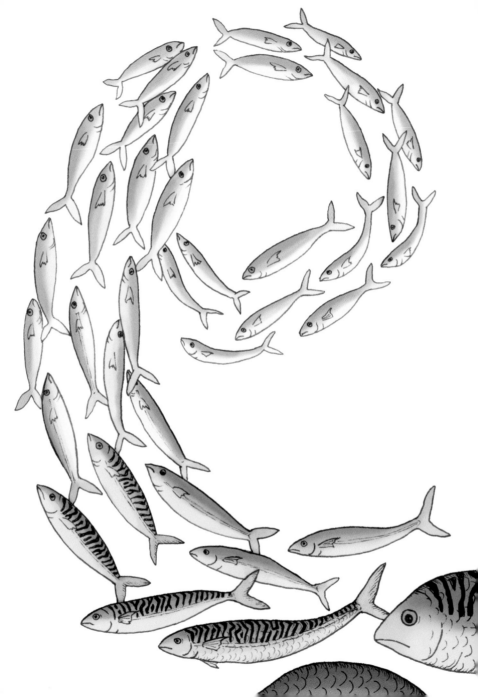

Just keep swimming

With a dappled blue and black streaked back, and a
silver belly beneath, mackerel are an attractive fish that
form enormous shoals several tens of thousands strong
in water close to the sea's surface. They are very fast
swimmers and must keep on swimming, day and night,
to take in oxygen from the water. As they keep moving,
mackerel do not have time to be choosy about what they
eat and will swallow up floating matter of most kinds.
Mackerel can live to be eighteen years old but are a
popular oily food fish for people and are fished heavily.

Keep things simple — very simple

∽

Jellyfish are a group of very primitive and simple animals, without a brain or heart, nor any form of skeleton. Lots have a round or bell-shaped body with a mouth and simple gut, and tentacles armed with stinging cells that hang in the water below. This simple anatomy has helped jellyfish thrive in all the world's oceans, from the tropics to the poles, and from surface waters to the very deep sea. Some jellyfish have a very powerful sting, and while they are best not touched, they are beautiful, very varied in form, and mesmerizing to watch.

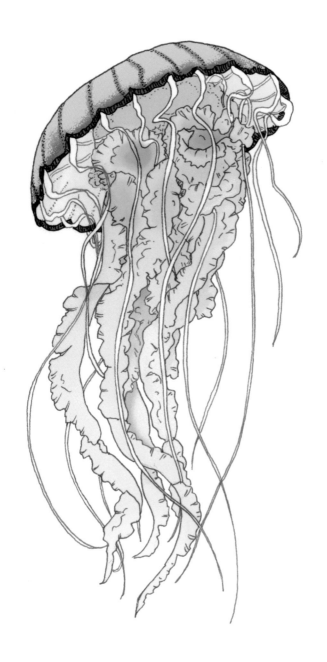

Avoid clutter

∞

Finding and watching wildlife needs an inquisitive mind
and patience, but very little equipment. You don't even
need to get your feet wet! With waterproof binoculars
you can see whales and dolphins. A shallow tray, to
temporarily house small animals before returning them
to the water, is helpful for shore study. More equipment,
along with in-depth training, is essential for scuba diving,
but a mask and snorkel are all you need for a surprisingly
similar and rewarding experience. When observing
wildlife, generally speaking, it is best to look and not to
touch, avoid trying to move animals and seaweeds stuck
to rocks, and leave things exactly as you found them.

Rediscover the colour of youth

~

While the sea sometimes seems too cold to take a dip in, the shallow waters around cooler seasonal coasts teem with life in summer and it's worth taking the plunge. Just a few feet offshore, there are nursery areas for flatfish, wrasses and cod-like pollack – in youth, these fish can be very colourful, in shades and patterns that are lost when the fish mature. Don a mask and snorkel to discover this bright world of life – the range of sea urchins, starfish, crabs and sea squirts adds to the mesmerizing and addictive array of life you can see.

Even scary things need to be protected

∞

The blue shark is an ocean-going wanderer. It is
beautifully proportioned, and coloured a sleek and
shiny silver-blue. It is a fast swimmer whose main
prey is squid and small fish, although it isn't above
eating carrion, and a keen sense of smell helps it find
the occasional feast that a recently deceased whale
offers. Blue shark is a popular food for people, and its
fins are used for soup in some places, meaning it is
one of the most heavily fished of sharks and is now a
threatened species. Please leave shark off your menu.

One individual's waste is another's treasure

༄

Very little goes to waste in the ocean, but some debris
falls from sunlit surface waters into deeper water. This
falling material, composed of decaying animals, fish scales
and excreted waste products is known as marine snow,
dropping slowly but steadily on its way to the sea floor.
Much is picked off by scavenging creatures like shrimps,
snails and many more. If this snow gets to the seabed,
nutrients will be locked in sediments until strong currents
move them on, taking them to other parts of the ocean
– they may return to the surface in upwellings on the
coast. The ocean is one continuous recycling system.

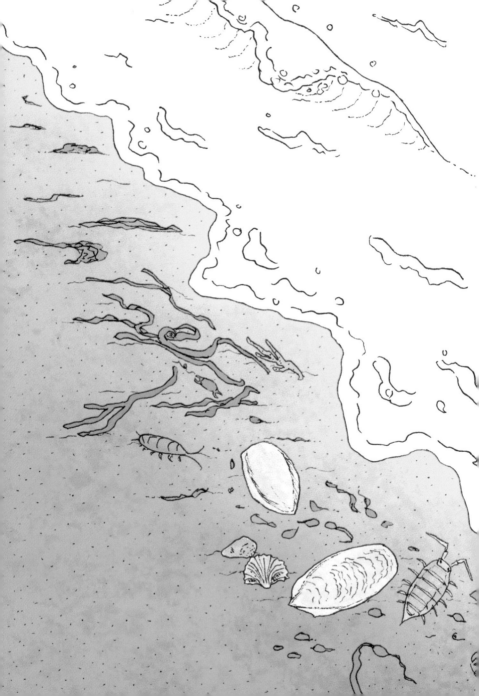

Enjoy the treasures of the beach

∞

The sea leaves behind many of its treasures on the beach, in the form of a strandline of objects of many wondrous things. You can find shells, cuttlebones, mermaid's purses, along with lots of seaweed. Strandlines are a free gift for wildlife, lots of insects and pillbug-like sea slaters, which can feed on rotting weeds and animal remains. The sea also leaves behind egg cases, bones and shells and, sadly, often human trash as well. Items may have floated from far and wide, from distant oceans and continents; they all make for a fascinating search.

Set yourself up for a good night's sleep

Parrotfish have a peculiar way of setting themselves up for the night. In the shelter of a crevice, each fish will cover itself in a thick layer of mucous, which it produces from its mouth. Unsurprisingly, it seems that predators leave them alone, but the main benefit of this gloopy sleeping bag seems to be that it protects the fish from parasites that would otherwise bug it as it slept. Some parrotfish eat coral, biting off chunks of the living reef for food. The inedible part of the coral rock is excreted out by the fish in fine chunks – the fish are believed to supply large quantities of the sand that builds up on local beaches!

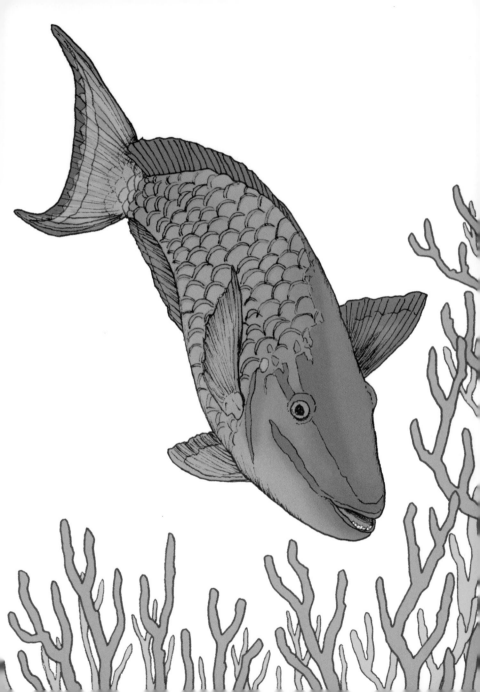

When you find a diet that works – stick to it

Blue whales are enormous, growing to over 100 feet long and weighing more than any animal known to have existed. They are able to grow so big by feeding almost entirely on krill, small shrimp-like creatures that are common in oceanic waters. The blue whale can scoop an entire swarm of many thousands of krill into its enormous mouth in just one gulp. The Southern Ocean, around Antarctica, is very rich in krill, and several kinds of whale, including blue whales, migrate there just to fill up on this nutritious feast.

Live life on the edge

A hydrothermal vent is a volcano-like crack in the sea
floor, giving out heated seawater and chemicals from
molten rocks lying beneath. Life abounds in these places,
but with a surprising twist: rather than plant plankton
and photosynthesis being the source of food for animals
here, the bacteria make their energy using minerals and
chemicals in the water, in a process called chemosynthesis.
Animals that are found nowhere else thrive here, including
giant tubeworms that host these bacteria in their body
tissues, and species of crabs and shrimps that tolerate
conditions here that are toxic to most sea creatures.

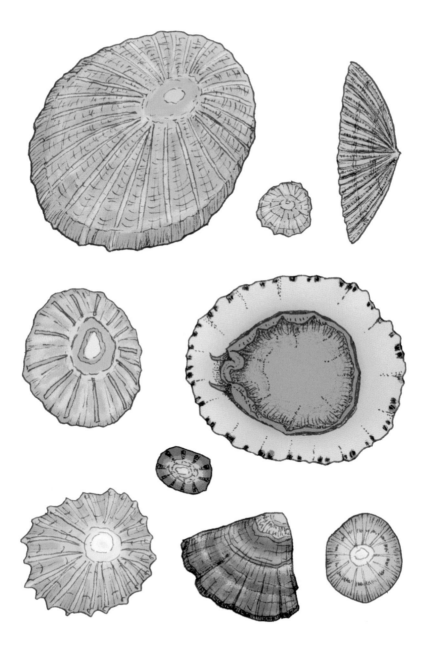

Make your home your own

〜

The common limpet is a familiar, cone-shaped shell seen stuck on rocky shores. It is usually coloured white, but it moves so slowly that it often finds itself covered in barnacles and seaweed. It does move, when the tide comes in, to graze on algae. It then returns to the same place (called its home scar) which is a mark on the rock on to which its shell fits very precisely. When it feeds, the limpet uses a tongue-like organ called a radula, which has tiny teeth on it, to rub away at rocks and weeds. These teeth are made from a material that is one of the hardest in nature, harder than many rocks.

It's OK to be boring

∞

Boring animals slowly work their way into rocks or timbers, usually to make a strong and secure home. The piddock is an unusual two-shelled mollusc, a little like a mussel. It uses its shell to rub away at soft rock, like chalk and loose sandstone, making a hollow tube to live in. You may find a piddock shell washed up on a beach and be surprised that the shells are quite thin and easily broken. If both shells are seen together, they look a little like wings, hence their alternative name of angel wings.

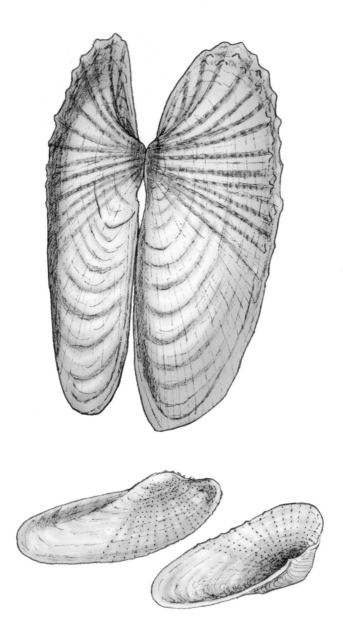

There are many gender-fluid fish in the sea

Wrasses are colourful fish, brightening up kelp forests
and reefs of coral or rock. There are lots of different
kinds, and several have an unusual way of making sure
there are enough males around to breed. More wrasse
are born female than male, but as they get bigger, and
when males become scarce, a female wrasse can turn
into a male. This happens surprisingly quickly – in just
twenty days for a blue-headed wrasse. Several kinds of
fish and other marine life are known to change sex, from
female to male or vice versa, and many are, or can become
hermaphrodite – the ocean is a fluid environment after all.

Variety is the spice of life

∞

Flatfish are bony fish with a flattened body which, when they are just little fry swimming among the plankton, look much like other fish do – with an eye on each side of the head. As the fish grows bigger, it goes through a twisting phase, so that both of its eyes sit on the one upper side of its body. The face of a flounder, plaice or sole looks quite comical up close, with an uncomfortable expression given by the twisted mouth – if you can find them, as they are so good at camouflaging and hiding in sand. They are not at all closely related to skates and rays, but all have evolved with flattened body shapes that make them great seabed hunters.

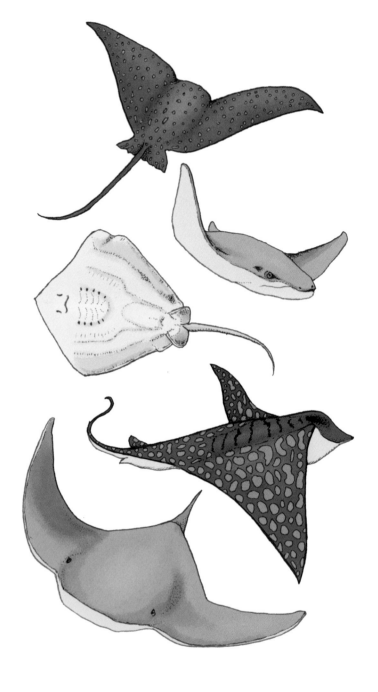

Use your senses to succeed

⌇

Skates and rays are fish with an ancient lineage and,
like sharks, have skeletons made of cartilage, not bone.
Most live close to the sea floor, and several have sensitive
receptors near the snout and mouth that pick up
electrical pulses from animals buried in sand, which they
can dig out and eat. The enormous manta is different,
swimming gracefully through surface waters to eat up
plankton. Many skates and rays can grow very big, like
the common skate – you may find an enormous egg
case, over twenty centimetres long, washed up on a
beach in spring – these are known as mermaid's purses,
from which a young skate will have hatched at sea.

History is all around you

∞

Sea squirts are not very impressive-looking creatures, but they are believed to be closer in evolutionary ancestry to us than most other animals without a backbone. This is because the sea squirts have a nervous system when they are in their plankton larval form similar to that seen in developing embryos of humans, birds, reptiles and fish. It is easy to think of evolution as being a steady advance from simple forms to complicated ones over time, but so many species, like the sea squirts, are adept and evolved to thrive in the sea just as they are. The light bulb sea squirt, mostly transparent, appears to reflect brightly when exposed to light with white lines resembling a filament in an old electrical light bulb.

Be flamboyant

∽

Nothing beats the cuttlefish for style and colour. With
a big brain and keen eyes that can see widely around
them, cuttles are cute creatures, able to hide and hunt
with an instantly changeable skin colour and pattern.
The flamboyant cuttlefish can change its form and
shape to look like a completely different creature in
an extraordinary range of colours, like lipstick pink,
purples and blues. A cuttlefish is kept buoyed up by
a white bonelike structure, which outlasts the soft
body tissues after death and will float undamaged for
many months and often wash up on the shore.

Index

Anemone
p. 82

Anglerfish
p. 18

Atlantic
cod p. 88

Atlantic
salmon p. 84

Barnacle
p. 28

Basking
shark p. 70

Bass
p. 42

Blue shark
p. 100

Blue whale
p. 108

Bottlenose
dolphin p. 90

Christmas tree
worm p. 44

Clownfish,
anemone p. 54

Common
blenny p. 14

Common
limpet p. 112

Common
starfish p. 32

Cone shell
p. 86

Coral
p. 26

Crab, lobster
p. 80

Cuttlefish
p. 125

Flatfish
p. 118

Flying
squid p. 36

Giant kelp
p. 76

Grey seal
p. 56

Gulper
eel p. 64

Harlequin
snake eel *p.38*

Humpback
whale *p.50*

Hydrothermal
vent *p.110*

Jellyfish
p.94

Killer whale
p.74

Leafy sea
dragon *p.62*

Leatherback
turtle *p.66*

Light bulb sea
squirt *p.122*

Lumpfish
p.40

Mackerel
p.92

Marine
iguana *p.68*

Marine
snow *p.102*

Moss animals
p.10

Narwhal
p.16

Ocean
quahog *p.48*

Octopus
p.58

Parrotfish
p.106

Piddick
p.114

Plant
plankton *p.6*

Seagrass
p.22

Seahorse
p.60

Sea otter
p.78

Sea slug
p.46

Seaweed
p.20

Skate
p.120

Snapping
shrimp *p.24*

Sperm
whale *p.52*

Sponge
p.12

Strandline
p.104

Wrasse
p.72, 116

About the author

RICHARD HARRINGTON is a marine biologist and writer. A regular contributor to *Coast Magazine* in the UK, he has been consulted on several documentaries such as the BBC's *Blue Planet 2* and *Blue Planet UK*, *Sky Ocean Rescue*, and the feature *The End of the Line*. He previously worked for the Marine Conservation Society and is currently the Head of Communications and Fundraising for Bees for Development. He loves to explore life between the tides.

About the illustrator

ANNIE DAVIDSON is an Australian illustrator based in Melbourne. She works across different mediums but predominantly with fineliner pen and digital colour to produce joyful, vibrant and detailed works. Her illustrations have appeared in books, on textiles, shop windows, wall stickers, in art exhibitions and for various clients worldwide including Lonely Planet, Converse, and the Melbourne Museum, to name a few.